Grandpa's Naughty Joke Book

Regarding The Jokes

Neither dirty jokes nor foul language per sé
But some of these jokes are very **risque!**

The jokes in this book are part of a collection of
over 6,000 jokes and quotations the author has
accumulated.

**Carey is one of the largest publishers of
joke books on the internet.**

We make fun of everyone

Boys – Girls - Gays – Lesbians – Politicians -
Democrats – Republicans – Presidents -
Whites – Blacks – Browns – Yellows.

You all are going to get it !!!!!!!
~
If you have issues regarding morals and risque
jokes, please don't buy this book.
~

1

Two guys die in a car accident and an angel descends from heaven.
"I am to give you your wings so you can fly to heaven. But if you think one dirty thought or act out one dirty act your wings will fall off."

So they fly to heaven without any trouble but when they get there the first guy sees a naked woman walk by so his wings fall off. When he bends over to pick them up the second guy's wings fall off.

~~~~~~~~~~

Once a lady wanted to leave the U.S.A. but couldn't get a visa. One day, she met a man who told her not to dispair.

"I'll let you sneak aboard my captain's ship and take you to France, but you have to screw me every time I bring you food, okay?"

She accepted, and for about three months the guy brought her food and water and then she screwed him. This went on for about 3 months, at which point she was discovered by the captain. The captain asked what she was doing and she said a man was taking her to France if she screwed him every time he brought her food.

The captain replied, "He sure is screwing you - this is the New York Ferry."

~~~~~~~~~~

A man was having problems with premature ejaculation so he decided to go to the doctor. He asked the doctor what he could do to cure his problem. In response, the doctor said: "When you feel like you are getting ready to ejaculate, try startling yourself."

That same day the man went to the store and bought himself a starter pistol. All excited to try this suggestion, he ran home to his wife. At home, he found his wife was in bed, naked and waiting. As the two began, they found themselves in the 69 position. The man, moments later, felt the sudden urge to ejaculate, so he fired the starter pistol.

The next day, the man went back to the doctor.

"How did it go?" the doctor asked.

"Not that well," the man responded: "When I fired the pistol, my wife peed in my face, bit three inches off my penis and my neighbor came out of the closet with his hands in the air!"

~~~~~~~~~~

A blond city girl named Amy marries a Colorado rancher.

One morning, on his way out to check on the cows, the rancher says to Amy,

'The insemination man is coming over to impregnate one of our cows today, so I drove a nail into the 2 by 4 just above where the cow's stall is in the barn. Please show him where the cow is when he gets here, OK?'

The rancher leaves for the fields. After a while, the artificial insemination man arrives and knocks on the front door.

Amy takes him down to the barn. They walk along the row of cows and when Amy sees the nail, she tells him, 'This is the one right here.'

The man, assuming he is dealing with an air head blond, asks, 'Tell me lady, 'cause I'm dying to know; how would YOU know that this is the right cow to be bred?'

'That's simple," she said. "By the nail that's over its stall,' she explains very confidently.

Laughing rudely at her, the man says, 'And what, pray tell, is the nail for?'

The blond turns to walk away and says sweetly over her shoulder,

'I guess it's to hang your pants on.'

(It's nice to see a blond winning once in awhile.)

~~~~~~~~~~

4

Vat Da Hell, Ole ?

Ole's car was hit by a truck in an accident. In court, the trucking company's lawyer was questioning Ole.

'Didn't you say, sir, at the scene of the accident, 'I'm fine?' asked the lawyer.

Ole responded, 'Vell, I'll tell you vat happened. I had yust loaded my favorite mule, Bessie, into da.....'

'I didn't ask for any details', the lawyer interrupted. 'Just answer the question. Did you not say, at the scene of the accident, 'I'm fine'?

Ole said, 'Vell, I had yust got Bessie into da trailer and I vas driving down da road... ..

The lawyer interrupted again and said, 'Judge, I am trying to establish the fact that, at the scene of the accident, this man told the Highway Patrolman on the scene that he was just fine. Now several weeks after the accident he is trying to sue my client. I believe he is a fraud. Please tell him to simply answer the question.'

By this time, the Judge was fairly interested in Ole's answer and said to the lawyer, 'I'd like to hear what he has to say about his favorite mule, Bessie'.

Ole thanked the Judge and proceeded. 'Vell, as I vas saying, I had yust loaded Bessie, my favorite mule, into da trailer and vas driving her down da highvay ven dis huge semi-truck and trailer ran da stop sign and smacked my truck right in da side. I vas trown into one ditch and Bessie vas trown into da other. I vas hurting real bad and didn't vant to move. However, I could hear Bessie moaning and groaning. I knew she was in terrible shape yust by her groans'. 'Shortly after da accident da Highway Patrolman, he came to da scene.. He could hear Bessie moaning and groaning so he vent over to her'..

'After he looked at her and saw her fatal condition he took out his gun and shot her right 'tween da eyes.

Den da Patrolman, he came across da road, gun still smoking, looked at me and said, 'How are you feeling?'

'Now vat da hell vould YOU say?

~~~~~~~~~~

A man and his wife were having an argument about who should brew the coffee each morning.

The wife said, 'You should do it because you get up first, and then we don't have to wait as long to get our coffee.

The husband said, 'You are in charge of cooking around here and you should do it, because that is your job, and I can just wait for my coffee.'

Wife replies, 'No, you should do it, and besides, it is in the Bible that the man should do the coffee.'

Husband replies, 'I can't believe that, show me
'
So she fetched the Bible, and opened the New Testament and showed him at the top of several pages, that it indeed says 'HEBREWS'

~~~~~~~~~~

A couple drove down a country road for several miles, not saying a word.

An earlier discussion had led to an argument and neither of them wanted to concede their position.

As they passed a barnyard of mules, goats, and pigs, the husband asked sarcastically, 'Relatives of yours?'

'Yep,' the wife replied, 'in-laws.'

~~~~~~~~~~

While attending a Marriage Seminar dealing with communication,

Tom and his wife Grace listened to the instructor,

'It is essential that husbands and wives know

each other's likes and dislikes.'

He addressed the man,

'Can you name your wife's favorite flower?'

Tom leaned over, touched his wife's arm gently and whispered, 'It's Pillsbury, isn't it?

~~~~~~~~~~

When Love Fades.......

A man was sitting on the sofa watching TV when he heard his wife's voice from the kitchen.

What would you like for dinner Love? Chicken, beef or lamb?

He said, "Thank you, I'll have chicken."

Not you, you're having soup. I was talking to the cat."

~~~~~~~~~~

An elderly man really took care of his body. He lifted weights and jogged six miles every day. One morning he looked into the mirror, admiring his body, and noticed that he was suntanned all over with the exception of his tocky. So he decided to do something about that.

He went to the beach, undressed completely,

and buried himself in the sand, except for his penis, which he left sticking out of the sand.

A bit later, two little old ladies came strolling along the beach, one using a cane to help her get along. Upon seeing the thing sticking out of the sand, the lady with the cane began to move the penis around with her cane.

Remarking to the other little old lady, she said, 'There really is no justice in the world.'

The other little old lady asked, 'What do you mean by that?'

The first little old lady replied, 'Look at that. When I was 20, I was curious about it. When I was 30, I enjoyed it. When I was 40, I asked for it. When I was 50, I paid for it. When I was 60, I prayed for it. When I was 70, I forgot about it.

'Now that I' m 80, the damned things are growing wild, and I'm too old to squat.'

~~~~~~~~~~

'Some people ask the secret of our long marriage. We take time to go to a restaurant two times a week. A little candlelight, dinner, soft music and dancing. She goes Tuesdays, I go Fridays.'

~~~~~~~~~~

The Swede's wife stepped up to the tee and, as she bent over to place her ball, a gust of wind blew her skirt up and revealed her lack of underwear.

"Good God, woman! Why aren't you wearing any skivvies?", Ole demanded.

"Well, you don't give me enough housekeeping money to afford any," she replied.

The Swede immediately reached into his pocket and said, "For the sake of decency, here's a $50. Go and buy yourself some underwear.

Next, the Irishman's wife bent over to set her ball on the tee. Her skirt also blew up to show that she, too, is wearing no undies. "Blessed Virgin Mary, woman! You've no knickers. Why not?"

She replied, "I can't afford any on the little money you give me."

Patrick reached into his pocket and said, "For the sake of decency, here's a $20. Go out and buy yourself some underwear!"

Lastly, the Scotsman's wife bent over. The wind also took her skirt over her head to reveal that she, too, is naked.

"Sweet mudder of Jaysus, Aggie! Where the friggin hell are yer drawers?"

She too explained, 'You dinna give me enough money to be able at affarrd any."

The Scotsman reaches into his pocket and said, "Well, fer the love 'o decency, here's a comb. Tidy yerself up a bit.."

~~~~~~~~~~

A lady about 8 months pregnant got on a bus. She noticed the man opposite her was smiling at her. She immediately moved to another seat.

This time the smile turned into a grin, so she moved again. The man seemed more amused.

When on the fourth move, the man burst out laughing, she complained to the driver and he had the man arrested.

The case came up in court.

The judge asked the man, who was about 20 years old, what he had to say for himself.

The man replied, 'Well your Honor, it was like this: When the lady got on the bus, I couldn't help but notice her condition. She sat down under a sign that said, 'The Double Mint Twins are coming,' and I grinned. Then she moved and sat under a sign that said, 'Logan's Liniment will reduce the swelling,' and I had to smile.

Then she placed herself under a deodorant sign that said, 'William's Big Stick Did the Trick,' and I could hardly contain myself.

But, Your Honor, when she moved the fourth time and sat under a sign that said, 'Goodyear Rubber could have prevented this Accident!'.. I just lost it.'

'CASE DISMISSED!!

~~~~~~~~~~

A foursome of guys is waiting at the men's tee, while another foursome of women is hitting off from the ladies' tees.

The ladies are taking their time. When the final lady is ready to hit off, she hacks the ball about ten feet.. She goes over to it, lines it up, takes an almighty swing and misses it completely.

Then she hacks it another ten feet and finally hacks it another five feet, quietly cursing under her breath.

She glances up at the patiently waiting men and snarls, "I guess all those fu **# lessons I took over the winter didn't help one little bit."

One of the men immediately responds, "Well, there you have it; you should have taken golf lessons instead!!"

~~~~~~~~~~

For any of you who frequent restaurants and understand the need for the service to be faster, this short story is a timeless lesson on how consultants can make a difference to an organization...

Last week, we took some friends out to a new restaurant and noticed that the waiter who took our order carried a spoon in his shirt pocket.

It seemed a little strange. When another waiter brought our water, I noticed he also had a spoon in his shirt pocket.

Then I looked around and saw that all the staff had spoons in their pockets.

When the waiter came back to serve our soup I asked, 'Why the spoon?'

'Well', he explained, 'the restaurant's owners hired Andersen Consulting to revamp all our processes. After several months of analysis, they concluded that the spoon was the most frequently dropped utensil. It represents a drop frequency of approximately 3 spoons per table per hour. If our personnel are better prepared, we can reduce the number of trips back to the kitchen and save 15 man-hours per shift.'

As luck would have it, I dropped my spoon and he was able to replace it with his spare. 'I'll get another spoon next time I go to the kitchen, instead of making an extra trip to get it right now.'

I was impressed. I also noticed that there was a string hanging out of the waiter's fly.

Looking around, I noticed that all the waiters had the same string hanging from their flies.

So before he walked off, I asked the waiter, 'Excuse me, but can you tell me why you have that string right there?'

'Oh, certainly!' Then he lowered his voice.

'Not everyone is so observant. That consulting firm I mentioned also found out that we can save time in the restroom. By tying this string to the tip of you know what, we can pull it out without touching it and eliminate the need to wash our hands, shortening the time spent in the restroom by 76 percent.

I asked 'After you get it out, how do you put it back?'

'Well,' he whispered, 'I don't know about the others, but I use the spoon.'

~~~~~~~~~~

The train was quite crowded, and a U. S. Marine walked the entire length looking for a seat.

There seemed to be one next to a well-dressed, middle-aged, French woman, but when he got there, he saw it was taken by the woman's poodle.

The war-weary Marine asked, "Ma'am, may I have that seat?"

The French woman sniffed and said to no one in particular, "Americans are so rude. My little Fifi is using that seat.

The Marine walked the entire train again, but the only seat available was under that dog.

"Please, ma'am. May I sit down? I'm very tired."

She snorted, "Not only are you Americans rude, you are also arrogant!"

This time the Marine didn't say a word; he just picked up the little dog, tossed it out the train window, and sat down.

The woman shrieked, "Someone must defend my honor! Put this American in his place!"

An English gentleman sitting nearby spoke up. "Sir, you Americans seem to have a penchant for doing the wrong thing. You hold the fork in the wrong hand. You drive your autos on the wrong side of the road. And now, sir, you seem to have thrown the wrong bitch out the window."

~~~~~~~~~~

When U Black U Black:

This was written by a black gentleman in Texas. What a great sense of humor and creativity!!!

When I was born, I was BLACK ,

When I grew up, I was BLACK ,

When I went in the sun, I stayed BLACK,

When I got cold, I was BLACK ,

When I was scared, I was BLACK ,

When I was sick, I was BLACK ,

And when I die, I'll still be BLACK .

NOW, You 'white' folks...

When you're born, you're PINK,

When you grow-up, you're WHITE,

When you go in the sun, you get RED,

When you're cold, you turn BLUE,

When you're scared, you're YELLOW,

When you get sick, you're GREEN,

When you bruise, you turn PURPLE ,

And when you die, you look GRAY.

So who y'all callin' COLORED folks?

~~~~~~~~~~

That rarity in San Francisco , a
HETEROSEXUAL MAN, was lying in bed with
his new girlfriend.

After having great sex, she spent the next hour
just rubbing his testicles --something she really
seemed to enjoy.

As he was also enjoying it, he turned and
asked her, "Why do you love doing that?"

Because, she replied, "I miss mine."

~~~~~~~~~~

What Kids Know About the Ocean
Leave it to kids to share their writing skills &
thought process.

1) - This is a picture of an octopus. It has eight
testicles... (Kelly, age 6)

2) - Oysters' balls are called pearls. (Jerry, age
6)

3) - If you are surrounded by ocean you are an

Island .... If you don't have ocean all round you, you are incontinent. (Wayne , age 7)

4) - Sharks are ugly and mean, and have big teeth, just like Emily Richardson. She's not my friend any more. (Kylie, age 6)

5) - A dolphin breathes through an asshole on the top of its head. (Billy, age 8)

6) - My uncle goes out in his boat with 2 other men, a woman and some pots and comes back with crabs. (Millie, age 6)

7) - When ships had sails, they used to use the trade winds to cross the ocean. Sometimes when the wind didn't blow the sailors would whistle to make the wind come. My brother said they would have been better off eating beans. (William, age 7)

8) - Mermaids live in the ocean. I like mermaids. They are beautiful and I like their shiny tails, but how on earth do mermaids get pregnant? Like, really? (Helen, age 6)

9) - I'm not going to write about the ocean. My baby brother is always crying, my Dad keeps yelling at my Mom, and my big sister has just got pregnant, so I can't think what to write. (Amy, age 6)

10) - Some fish are dangerous. Jellyfish can sting. Electric eels can give you a shock. They have to live in caves under the sea where I think they have to plug themselves into

chargers at night. (Christopher, age 7)

11) - When you go swimming in the ocean, it is very cold, and it makes my willy small (Kevin, age 6)

12) - Divers have to be safe when they go under the water. Divers can't go down alone, so they have to go down on each other. (Becky, age 8)

13) - On vacation my Mom went water skiing. She fell off when she was going very fast. She says she won't do it again because water fired right up her big fat ass. (Julie, age 7)

14) - The ocean is made up of water and fish. Why the fish don't drown I don't know. (Bobby, age 6)

15) - My dad was a sailor on the ocean. He knows all about the ocean.. What he doesn't know is why he quit being a sailor and married my mom. (James, age 7)

~~~~~~~~~~

My neighbor found out her dog could hardly hear so she took it to the veterinarian. He found that the problem was hair in its ears. He cleaned both ears and the dog could hear fine. The vet then proceeded to tell the lady that if she wanted to keep this from recurring she should go to the store and get some "Nair" hair remover and rub it in the dog's ears once a month.

The lady goes to the drug store and gets some "Nair" hair remover. At the register the druggist tells her, "If you're going to use this under your arms don't use deodorant for a few days."
The lady says: "I'm not using it under my arms."

The druggist says: "If you're using it on your legs don't shave for a couple of days."
The lady says: "I'm not using it on my legs either; if you must know, I'm using it on my schnauzer.."

The druggist says: "Stay off your bicycle for at least a week."

~~~~~~~~~~~

A guy is driving around the back woods of Montana and he sees a sign in front of a broken down shanty-style house: 'Talking Dog For Sale ' He rings the bell and the owner, an attractive blonde, appears and tells him the dog is in the backyard.

The guy goes into the backyard and sees a nice looking Labrador retriever sitting there.

'You talk?' he asks.

'Yep,' the Lab replies.

After the guy recovers from the shock of hearing a dog talk, he says 'So, what's your story?'

The Lab looks up and says, 'Well, I discovered that I could talk when I was pretty young. I wanted to help the government, so I told the CIA. In no time at all they had me jetting from country to country, sitting in rooms with spies and world leaders, because no one figured a dog would be eavesdropping.'

'I was one of their most valuable spies for eight years running. But the jetting around really tired me out, and I knew I wasn't getting any younger so I decided to settle down. I signed up for a job at the airport to do some ndercover security, wandering near suspicious characters and listening in. I uncovered some incredible dealings and was awarded a batch of medals.' 'I got married, had a mess of puppies, and now I'm just retired.'

The guy is amazed. He goes back in and asks the blonde what she wants for the dog.

'Ten dollars,' the blonde says.

'Ten dollars? This dog is amazing! Why on earth are you selling him so cheap?'

'Because he's a liar. He never did any of that shit.

~~~~~~~~~~

A farmer stopped by the local mechanic shop to have his truck fixed. They couldn't do it while he waited, so he said he didn't live far and would just walk home.

On the way he stopped at the hardware store and bought a bucket and a gallon of paint. He then stopped by the feed store and picked up a couple of chickens and a goose.

However, struggling outside the store he now had a problem - how to carry his entire purchases home.

While he was scratching his head he was approached by a little old lady who told him she was lost. She asked, "Can you tell me how to get to 1603 Mockingbird Lane?"

The farmer said, "Well, as a matter of fact, my farm is very close to that house. I would walk you there, but I can't carry this lot."

The old lady suggested, "Why don't you put the can of paint in the bucket. Carry the bucket in one hand, put a chicken under each arm and carry the goose in your other hand?"

"Why, thank you very much, he said, and proceeded to walk the old girl home. On the way he says, "Let's take a short cut and go down this alley. We'll be there in no time."

The little old lady looked him over cautiously, then said, "I am a lonely widow without a husband to defend me.

How do I know that when we get in the alley you won't hold me up against the wall, pull up my skirt, and have your way with me?"

The farmer said, "Holy smokes lady! I'm carrying a bucket, a gallon of paint, two chickens and a goose. How in the world could I possibly hold you up against the wall and do that?"

The old lady replied, "Set the goose down, cover him with the bucket, put the paint on top of the bucket, and I'll hold the chickens...."

~~~~~~~~~~~

A man goes to a psychiatrist and says, "Doc, I think I'm gay."

The psychiatrist asks, "Why do you think your gay?"

"Because my grandfather is gay."

"Well, just because your grandfather is gay, doesn't mean you're gay."

"But my father is gay, too!"

"Well, just because your grandfather is gay and your father is gay, doesn't mean you're gay."

"But my brother is gay, too!"

The psychiatrist looks at him and says, "Isn't there anybody in your family who likes women?"

"Yeah, I think my sister does!"

~~~~~~~~~~

The following was found posted <u>very low</u> on a refrigerator door.

Dear Dogs and Cats:
The dishes with the paw prints are yours and contain your food. The other dishes are mine and contain my food. Placing a paw print in the middle of my plate and food does not stake a claim for it becoming your food and dish, nor do I find that aesthetically pleasing in the slightest.

The stairway was not designed by NASCAR and is not a racetrack. Racing me to the bottom is not the object. Tripping me doesn't help because I fall faster than you can run.

I cannot buy anything bigger than a king sized bed. I am very sorry about this. Do not think I will continue sleeping on the couch to ensure your comfort, however…dogs and cats can actually curl up in a ball when they sleep. It is not necessary to sleep perpendicular to each other, stretched out to the fullest extent possible. I also know that sticking tails straight out and having tongues hanging out on the other end to maximize space is nothing but sarcasm.

For the last time, there is no secret exit from the bathroom! If, by some miracle, I beat you there and manage to get the door shut, it is not necessary to claw, whine, meow, or try to turn the knob or get your paw under the edge in an attempt to open the door. I must exit through the same door I entered. Also, I have been using the bathroom for years - canine/feline attendance is not required.

The proper order for kissing is: Kiss me first, then go smell the other dog or cat's butt. I cannot stress this enough.

Finally, in fairness, dear pets, I have posted the following message on the front door:

TO ALL NON-PET OWNERS WHO VISIT AND LIKE TO COMPLAIN ABOUT OUR PETS:
(1) They live here. You don't.
(2) If you don't want their hair on your clothes, stay off the furniture. That's why they call it 'fur'-niture.
(3) I like my pets a lot better than I like most people.
(4) To you, they are animals. To me, they are adopted sons/daughters who are short, hairy, walk on all fours and don't speak clearly.

Remember, dogs and cats are better than kids because they:
(1) eat less,

(2) don't ask for money all the time,
(3) are easier to train,
(4) normally come when called,
(5) never ask to drive the car,
(6) don't smoke or drink,
(7) don't want to wear your clothes,
(8) don't have to buy the latest fashions,
(9) don't need a gazillion dollars for college and
(10) if they get pregnant, you can sell their children...

~~~~~~~~~~

Dear Ma and Pa,

I am well. Hope you are. Tell Brother Walt and Brother Elmer the Marine Corps beats working for old man Minch by a mile. Tell them to join up quick before all of the places are filled.

I was restless at first because you get to stay in bed till nearly 6 a.m. But I am getting so I like to sleep late. Tell Walt and Elmer all you do before breakfast is smooth your cot, and shine somethings. No hogs to slop, feed to pitch, mash to mix, wood to split, fire to lay. Practically nothing.

Men got to shave but it is not so bad, there's warm water.

Breakfast is strong on trimmings like fruit juice, cereal, eggs, bacon, etc., but kind of weak on chops, potatoes, ham, steak, fried eggplant, pie and other regular food, but tell Walt and Elmer you can always sit by the two city boys that live on coffee.Their food, plus yours, holds you until noon when you get fed again. It's no wonder these city boys can't walk much.

We go on 'route marches,' which the platoon sergeant says are long walks to harden us. If he thinks so, it's not my place to tell him different. A 'route march' is about as far as to our mailbox at home. Then the city guys get sore feet and we all ride back in trucks.

The sergeant is like a school teacher. He nags a lot. The Captain is like the School Board. Majors and colonels just ride around and frown.They don't bother you none.

This next will kill Walt and Elmer with laughing. I keep getting medals for shooting. I don't know why. The bulls-eye is near as big as a chipmunk head and don't move, and it ain't shooting at you like the Higgett boys at home. All you got to do is lie there all comfortable and hit it. You don't even load your own cartridges they come in boxes.

Then we have what they call hand-to-hand combat training. You get to wrestle with them city boys. I have to be real careful though, they break real easy. It ain't like fighting with that ole bull at home. I'm about the best they got in this except for that Tug Jordan from over in Silver Lake. I only beat him once. He joined up the same time as me, but I'm only 5'6' and 130 pounds and he's 6'8' and near 300 pounds dry.

Be sure to tell Walt and Elmer to hurry and join before other fellers get onto this setup and come stampeding in.

Your loving daughter,

Alice

~~~~~~~~~~

Lynn and Judy were doing some carpenter work on a Habitat for Humanity House. Lynn was nailing down house siding, would reach into her nail Pouch, pull out a nail and either toss it over her shoulder or nail it In.

Judy, figuring this was worth looking into, asked, 'Why are you throwing those nails away?' Lynn explained, 'When I pull a nail out of my pouch, about half of them have the head on the wrong end and I throw them away.' Judy got completely upset and yelled, You moron! Those nails aren't Defective! They're for the other side of the house!'

~~~~~~~~~~

A guy calls his buddy, the horse rancher, and says he's sending a friend over to look at a horse.

His buddy asks, 'How will I recognize him?'

'That's easy; he's a midget with a speech

impediment.'

So, the midget shows up, and the guy asks him if he's looking for a male or female horse.

'A female horth.'

So he shows him a prized filly.

'Nith lookin horth. Can I thee her eyeth'?

So the guy picks up the midget and he gives the horse's eyes the once over.

'Nith eyeth, can I thee her earzth'?

So he picks the little fella up again, and shows him the horse's ears..

'Nith earzth, can I see her mouf'?

The rancher is getting pretty ticked off by this point, but he picks him up again and shows him the horse's mouth.

'Nice mouf, can I see her twat'?

Totally mad as fire at this point, the rancher grabs him under his arms and rams the midget's head as far as he can up the horse's fanny, pulls him out and slams him on the ground.

The midget gets up, sputtering and coughing.

'Perhapth I should rephrase that.

Can I thee her wun awound a widdlebit'?

~~~~~~~~~~

INNOCENCE IS PRICELESS

One Sunday morning, the pastor noticed little Alex standing in the foyer of the church staring up at a large plaque . It was covered with names and small flags mounted on either side of it. The six-year old had been staring at the plaque for some time, so the pastor walked up, stood beside the little boy, and said quietly, "Good morning, Alex."

"Good morning Pastor," he replied, still focused on the plaque. "Pastor, what is this?"

The pastor said, "Well, son, it's a memorial to all the young men and women who died in the service."

Soberly, they just stood together, staring at the large plaque. Finally, little Alex's voice, barely audible and trembling with fear, asked,

"Which service, the 8:30 or the 10:30 ?"

~~~~~~~~~~

Have you noticed that stairs are getting *steeper* Groceries are *heavier* . And, everything is *farther* away. Yesterday I walked to the corner and I was dumbfounded to discover how *long* our street had become! Another thing, they're putting something in the water; I am getting taller and can't reach my feet anymore!

And, you know, people are less considerate now, especially the young ones. They speak in *whispers* all the time! If you ask them to speak up they just keep repeating themselves, endlessly mouthing the same *silent message* until they're red in the face! What do they think I am a lip reader?

I also think they are much younger than I was at the same age. On the other hand, people my own age are so much *older* than I am. I ran into an old friend the other day and she has aged so much that *she didn't even recognize* me!

I got to thinking about the poor dear as I was combing my hair this morning, and in doing so, glanced at my own reflection. well, REALLY NOW - even mirrors are not made the way they used to be!

Another thing, everyone drives so fast these days! You're risking life and limb if you happen to pull onto the freeway in front of them. All I can say is, their brakes must wear out awfully fast, the way I see them screech and swerve in my rear view mirror.

Clothing manufacturers are less civilized these days. Why else would they suddenly start labeling a size 10 or 12 dress as 18 or 20? Do they think no one notices? The people who make bathroom scales are pulling the same prank. Do they think I actually 'believe' the number I see on that dial? HA! I would never let myself weigh that much! Just who do these people think they're fooling?

I'd like to call up someone in authority to report what's going on -- but the telephone company is in on the conspiracy too: they've printed the phone books in such small type that no one could ever find a number in there! All I can do is pass along this warning:

WE ARE UNDER ATTACK!

Unless something drastic happens, pretty soon everyone will have to suffer these awful indignities.

~~~~~~~~~~

The phone rings and the lady of the house answers.

"Hello?"

"Mrs. King, please."

"Speaking."

"Mrs. King, this is Dr. Jones at the hospital laboratory. When your husband's doctor sent his biopsy to the lab last week, a biopsy from another Mr. King arrived as well. We are now uncertain which one belongs to your husband. Frankly, either way the results are not too good."

"What do you mean?" Mrs. King asks nervously.

"Well, one of the specimens tested positive for Alzheimer's and the other one tested positive for HIV. We can't tell which is which."

"That's dreadful! Can you do the test again?" questioned Mrs. King.

"Normally we can, but the new health care system will only pay for these expensive tests one time."

'Well, what am I supposed to do now? "

"The folks at Obama health care recommend that you drop your husband off somewhere in the middle of town. If he finds his way home, don't sleep with him."

~~~~~~~~~~~

A cop in TN. was driving down the road and ran out of gas. Just at that moment, a bee flew in his window. The bee said, 'What seems to be the problem?' 'I'm out of gas,' the cop replied.

The bee told the cop to wait right there and flew away. Minutes later, the man watched as an entire swarm of bees flew to his car and into his gas tank. After a few minutes, the bees flew out.

'Try it now,' said one bee. The cop turned the ignition key and the car started right up. 'Wow!' the cop exclaimed, 'what did you put in my gas tank'?

BP

~~~~~~~~~~~

Bubba and Billy Joe are walking down the street in Atlanta and they see a sign on a store which reads, "Suits $5.00 each, shirts $2.00 each, pants $2.50 each.

Bubba says to his pal, "Billy Joe, Look here! We could buy a whole gob of these, take 'em back to Mountain Home, sell 'em to our friends, and make
a fortune. Just let me do the talkin' 'cause if they hear your accent, they might think we're ignorant, and not wanna sell that stuff to us. Now, I'll
talk in a slow Georgia drawl so's they don't know we is from Arkansas."

They go in and Bubba says with his best fake Georgia drawl, "I'll take 50 of them suits at $5.00 each, 100 of them there shirts at $2.00 each, 50
pairs of them there pants at $2.50 each.
I'll back up my pickup and...."

The owner of the shop interrupts, "Ya'll from North Arkansas, ain't ya?"

"Well...yeah," says a surprised Bubba. "How come you knowed that?"

"Because this is a dry-cleaners."

~~~~~~~~~~

Two sisters, one blonde and one brunette, inherit the family ranch. Unfortunately, after just a few years, they are in financial trouble. In order to keep the bank from repossessing the ranch, they need to purchase a bull so that they can breed their own stock.

Upon leaving, the brunette tells her sister, 'When I get there, if I decide to buy the bull, I'll contact you to drive out after me and haul it home.' The brunette arrives at the man's ranch, inspects the bull, and decides she wants to buy it. The man tells her that he will sell it for $599, no less.

After paying him, she drives to the nearest town to send her sister a telegram to tell her the news. She walks into the telegraph office, and says, "I want to send a telegram to my sister telling her that I've bought a bull for our ranch. I need her to hitch the trailer to our pickup truck and drive out here so we can haul it home."

The telegraph operator explains that he'll be glad to help her, then adds, it will cost 99 cents a word.

Well, after paying for the bull, the brunette realizes that she'll only be able to send her sister one word.
After a few minutes of thinking, she nods and says, 'I want you to send her the word 'comfortable.'

The operator shakes his head. "How is she ever going to know that you want her to hitch the trailer to your pickup truck and drive out here to haul that bull back to your ranch if you send her just the word 'comfortable?"

The brunette explains, "My sister's blonde. The word is big. She'll read it very slowly....

'com-for-da-bul."

~~~~~~~~~~

"In my many years I have come to a conclusion that one useless man is a shame, two is a law firm and three or more is a congress."

John Adams

~~~~~~~~~~

Beats Me !!

1. Is it good if a vacuum really sucks?

2. Why is the third hand on the watch called the second hand?

3. If a word is misspelled in the dictionary, how

would we ever know?

4. If Webster wrote the first dictionary, where did he find the words?

5. Why do we say something is out of whack? What is a whack?

6. Why does "slow down" and "slow up" mean the same thing?

7. Why does "fat chance" and "slim chance" mean the same thing?

8. Why do "tug" boats push their barges?

9. Why do we sing "Take me out to the ball game" when we are already there?

10. Why are they called "stands" when they are made for sitting?

11. Why is it called "after dark" when it really is "after light"?

12. Doesn't "expecting the unexpected" make the unexpected expected?

13. Why are a "wise man" and a "wise guy" opposites?

14. Why do "overlook" and "oversee" mean opposite things?

15. Why is "phonics" not spelled the way it sounds?

16. If work is so terrific, why do they have to pay you to do it?

17. If all the world is a stage, where is the audience sitting?

18. If love is blind, why is lingerie so popular?

19. If you are cross-eyed and have dyslexia, can you read all right?

20. Why is bra singular and panties plural?

21. Why do you press harder on the buttons of a remote control when you know the batteries are dead?

22. Why do we put suits in garment bags and garments in a suitcase?

23. How come abbreviated is such a long word?

24. Why do we wash bath towels? Aren't we clean when we use them?

25. Why doesn't glue stick to the inside of the bottle?

26. Why do they call it a TV set when you only have one?

27. Why do we drive on a parkway and park on a driveway?

29.   Why is toilet paper tiny squares and tissues big squares?

~~~~~~~~~~

Did you hear about the two blondes who froze to death in a drive-in movie?

They had gone to see 'Closed for the Winter.'

~~~~~~~~~~

John was a salesman's delight when it came to any kind of unusual gimmicks. His wife Marsha had long ago given up trying to get him to change.

One day John came home with another one of his unusual purchases. It was a robot that John claimed was actually a lie detector.

It was about 5:30 that afternoon when Tommy, their 11 year old son, returned home from school. Tommy was over 2 hours late.
"Where have you been? Why are you over 2 hours late getting home?" asked John.
"Several of us went to the library to work on an extra credit project," said Tommy.

The robot immediately walked around the table and slapped Tommy, knocking him completely out of his chair.
"Son," said John, "this robot is a lie detector, now tell us where you really were after school."

"We went to Bobby's house and watched
a movie." said Tommy.
"What did you watch?" asked Marsha.
"The Ten Commandments." answered
Tommy.

The robot went around to Tommy and once
again slapped him, knocking him off his chair.
With his lip quivering, Tommy got up, sat down
and said..."I am sorry I lied.   We really
watched a tape called Sex Queen."

"I am ashamed of you son," said John. "When
I was your age I never lied to my parents."

The robot walked around to John and delivered
a whack that nearly knocked him out of his
chair. Marsha doubled over in laughter, almost
in tears and said, "Boy, did you ever ask for
that one! You can't be too mad with Tommy.
After all, he is your son!"

The robot promptly walked around to Marsha
and knocked her out of her chair.

~~~~~~~~~~~

BEER BY SEVEN YEAR OLDS

 A handful of 7 year old children were asked
'What they thought of beer'.
Some interesting responses, but the last one is
especially good.

'I think beer must be good. My dad says the

more beer he drinks the prettier my mom gets.'
--Tim, 7 years old

'Beer makes my dad sleepy and we get to
watch what we want on television when he is
asleep, so beer is nice. '
--Mellanie, 7 years old

'My Mom and Dad both like beer. My Mom gets
funny when she drinks it and takes her top off
at parties, but Dad doesn't think this is very
funny.'
--Grady, 7 years old

"My Mom and Dad talk funny when they drink
beer and the more they drink the more they
give kisses to each other, which is a good
thing.'
--Toby, 7 years old

'My Dad gets funny on beer. He is funny. He
also wets his pants sometimes, so he shouldn't
have too much.
--Sarah, 7 years old

'My Dad loves beer. The more he drinks, the
better he dances. One time he danced right
into the pool.'
--Lilly, 7 years old

'I don't like beer very much. Every time Dad
drinks it, he burns the sausages on the
barbecue and they taste disgusting.'
--Ethan, 7 years old

'I give Dad's beer to the dog and he goes to sleep.'
--Shirley, 7 years old

'My Mom drinks beer and she says silly things and picks on my father. Whenever she drinks beer she yells at Dad and tells him to go bury his bone down the street again, but that doesn't make any sense.'
--Jack, 7 years

~~~~~~~~~~

How true it is today

'If you don't read the newspaper you are uninformed, if you do read the newspaper you are misinformed.'
-Mark Twain

~~~~~~~~~~

Jeff Gordon fires entire pit crew!

This announcement followed Gordon's decision to take advantage of President Obama's proposal to employ Harlem youngsters.

The decision to hire them was brought about by a recent documentary on how unemployed youths from Harlem were able to remove a set of wheels in less than 6 seconds without proper equipment, whereas Gordon's existing crew could only do it in 8 seconds with millions of dollars worth of high tech equipment.

It was thought to be an excellent and bold move by Gordon's management team as most races are won or lost in the pits.

At the crew's first practice session, not only was the inexperienced crew able to change all 4 wheels in under 6 seconds, but within 12 seconds they had changed the paint scheme, altered the VIN number, and sold the car to Dale Jr. for 10 cases of Bud, a bag of weed, and some photos of Jeff Gordon's wife in the shower.

~~~~~~~~~~

A blonde hurried into the emergency room late one night with the tip Of her index finger shot off. 'How did this happen?' the emergency Room doctor asked her.

'Well, I was trying to commit suicide,' the blonde replied.

'What?' sputtered the doctor. 'You tried to commit suicide by shooting Off your finger?'

'No, Silly' the blonde said. 'First I put the gun to my chest, and Then I thought, 'I just paid $6,000.00 for these implants..

I'm not shooting myself in the chest.'

'So then?' asked the doctor.

'Then I put the gun in my mouth, and I thought, 'I just paid $3,000.00 To get my teeth straightened I'm not shooting myself in the mouth.'

'So then?'

'Then I put the gun to my ear, and I thought: 'This is going to make a Loud noise. So I put my finger in my other ear before I pulled the Trigger.

~~~~~~~~~~

Q. What is the difference between a Drug Dealer and a Hooker?

A. A Hooker can wash her crack and sell it again.

Q. What's a mixed feeling?

A. When you see your Mother-In-Law backing off a cliff in your new Lexus.

Q. What's the height of conceit?

A. Having an orgasm and calling out your own name.

Q. What's the definition of 'Macho'?

A. Jogging home from your vasectomy.

Q. What's the difference between a G-Spot and a golf ball?

A. A guy will actually search for a golf ball

Q. Do you know how New Zealanders practice safe sex?

A. They spray paint X's on the back of the sheep that kick!

Q. Why is divorce so expensive?

A. Because it's worth it!

Q. What is a Yankee?

A. The same as a quickie, but a Guy can do it alone.

Q. What do Tupperware and a Walrus have in common?

A. They both like a tight seal.

Q. What do a Christmas tree and a Priest have in common?

A. Their balls are just for decoration.

Q. What is the difference between 'ooooooh'and 'aaaaaaah'?

A. About three inches.

Q: What's the difference between purple and

pink?

A. The grip.

Q. How do you find a Blind Man in a nudist colony?

A. It's not hard.

Q: What's the difference between a Girlfriend and a Wife?

A: 45 pounds.

Q: What's the difference between a Boyfriend and a Husband?

A: 45 minutes.

Q: Why do men find it difficult to make eye contact?

A: Breasts don't have eyes.

Q: What is the difference between medium and rare?

A: Six inches is medium, eight inches is rare.

Q. Why do women rub their eyes when they get up in the morning?

A. They don't have balls to scratch!

~~~~~~~~~~

From a retired medical professional:

Let me get this straight. Obama's health care plan will be written by a committee whose head says he doesn't understand it, passed by a Congress that hasn't read it, signed by a president who smokes, funded by a treasury chief who did not pay his taxes, overseen by a surgeon general who is obese, and financed by a country that is nearly broke.

What could possibly go wrong?

~~~~~~~~~~

A Greek and Italian were talking one day discussing who had the superior culture.
Over coffee the Greek says, "Well, we have the Parthenon."

The Italian replies, "We have the Coliseum."

The Greek retorts, "We Greeks gave birth to mathematics"

The Italian, nodding, says, "But we built the Roman Empire_."

And so on and so on until the Greek comes up with what he thinks will end the discussion. With a flourish of finality he says, "We invented sex!"

The Italian replies, "That is true, but it was the Italians who introduced it to women."

~~~~~~~~~~

A TRUE STORY FROM
THE HOUSTON HERALD NEWSPAPER
HOUSTON, TEXAS ~~ MARCH 5, 2009

Last Thursday night around midnight, a woman from Houston, Texas, was arrested, jailed and charged with manslaughter for shooting a man six times in the back as he was running away with her purse.

The following Monday morning, the woman was called in front of the arraignment judge, sworn in and asked to explain her actions.

The woman replied, "I was standing at the corner bus stop for about fifteen minutes, waiting for the bus to take me home after work. I am a waitress at a local cafe.

"I was alone there, so I had my hand on my pistol, that was in my purse, that was hung over my left shoulder. All of a sudden, I was being spun around hard to my left. As I caught my balance, I saw a man running away from me with my purse.

"I looked down at my right hand and I saw that my fingers were wrapped tightly around my pistol. The next thing I remember is saying out loud, No way, Punk! You're not stealing my pay check and tips. I raised my right hand, pointed my pistol at the man running away from me with my purse, and squeezed the trigger of my pistol six times!"

When asked by the arraignment judge, "Why did you shoot the man six times?" the woman replied under oath, "Because when I pulled the trigger of my pistol the seventh time, it only went click."

The woman was acquitted of all charges. And she was back at work at the cafe the next day!

Now, that's gun control.

~~~~~~~~~~

An Italian Confession

'Bless me Father, for I have sinned.
I have been with a loose girl'.

The priest asks, 'Is that you, little Joey Pagano ?'

'Yes, Father, it is.'

'And who was the girl you were with?'

'I can't tell you, Father. I don't want to ruin her reputation'.

"Well, Joey, I'm sure to find out her name sooner or later so you may as well tell me now. Was it Tina Minetti?'

'I cannot say.'

'Was it Teresa Mazzarelli?'

'I'll never tell.'

'Was it Nina Capelli?'

'I'm sorry, but I cannot name her.'

'Was it Cathy Piriano?'

'My lips are sealed.'

'Was it Rosa DiAngelo, then?'

'Please, Father, I cannot tell you.'

The priest sighs in frustration.
'You're very tight lipped, and I admire that.
But you've sinned and have to atone.
You cannot be an altar boy now for 4 months.
Now you go and behave yourself.'

Joey walks back to his pew, and his friend
Franco slides over and whispers, 'What'd you
get?'

'Four months vacation and five good leads.'

~~~~~~~~~~

A little boy was waiting for his mother to come
out of the grocery store. As he waited, he was
approached by a man who asked, "Son, can

you tell me where the Post Office is?"

The little boy replied, "Sure! Just go straight down this street a coupla blocks and turn to your right."

The man thanked the boy kindly and said, "I'm the new pastor in town. I'd like for you to come to church on Sunday. I'll show you how to get to Heaven."

The little boy replied with a chuckle. "Awww, come on... you don't even know the way to the Post Office."

~~~~~~~~~~

A blonde was driving home after a game and got caught in a really bad Hailstorm. Her car was covered with dents, so the next day she took it To a repair shop.. The shop owner saw that she was a blonde, so he Decided to have some fun.. He told her to go home and blow into the Tail pipe really hard, and all the dents would pop out.

So, the blonde went home, got down on her hands and knees and started Blowing into her tailpipe. Nothing happened.. So she blew a little Harder, and still nothing happened.

Her blonde roommate saw her and asked, 'What are you doing?' The first Blonde told her how the repairman had instructed her to blow into the Tail pipe in order to get all the dents to pop out. The roommate rolled her eyes and said, 'Uh, like hello! You need to roll up the windows first.'

~~~~~~~~~~

A Mafia Godfather finds out that his bookkeeper has cheated him out of ten million bucks. His bookkeeper is deaf. That was the reason he got the job in the first place.

It was assumed that a deaf bookkeeper would not hear anything that he might have to testify about in court.

When the Godfather goes to confront the bookkeeper about his missing $10 million, he brings along his attorney, who knows sign language.

The Godfather tells the lawyer, "Ask him where the 10 million bucks he embezzled from me is." The attorney, using sign language, asks the bookkeeper where the money is.

The bookkeeper signs back: "I don't know what you are talking about."

The attorney tells the Godfather: "He says he doesn't know what you're talking about."

The Godfather pulls out a pistol, puts it to the bookkeeper's temple and says, "Ask him again!"

The attorney signs to the bookkeeper: "He'll kill you if you don't tell him!"

The bookkeeper signs back: "OK! You win! The money is in a brown briefcase, buried behind the shed in my cousin Enzo's backyard in Queens!"

The Godfather asks the attorney: "Well, what'd he say?"

The attorney replies: "He says you don't have the cajones to pull the trigger."

~~~~~~~~~~~

Grandma and Grandpa were visiting their kids overnight. When Grandpa found a bottle of Viagra   his son's medicine cabinet, he asked about using one of the pills.

The son said, "I don't think you should take one Dad; they're very strong and very expensive."

"How much?" asked Grandpa.

"$10.00 a pill," Answered the son.

"I don't care," said Grandpa, "I'd still like to try one, and before we leave in the morning, I'll put the money under the pillow."

Later the next morning, the son found $110 under the pillow. He called Grandpa and said, "I told you each pill was $10, not $110.

"I know," said Grandpa. "The hundred is from Grandma!"

~~~~~~~~~~

Following a survey of men regarding oral sex, these were the conclusions:

3% liked the warmth
4% like the feeling
93% liked the quietness ☺

~~~~~~~~~

After numerous rounds of 'We don't even know if Osama bin Laden is still alive', Osama himself decided to send George Bush a letter in his own hand writing to let him know he was still in the game.

Bush opened the letter and it contained a single line of coded message:

370H-SSV-0773H

Bush was baffled, so he e-mailed it to Condoleezza Rice. Condi and her=2 0aides had not a
clue either, so they sent it to the FBI.

No one could solve it at the FBI so it went to the CIA, and then to MI6.

Eventually they asked the Mossad (Israeli intelligence) for help.

Within a minute Mossad emailed the White House with this reply:

'Tell the President he's holding the note upside down'

~~~~~~~~~~~

This is worrisome.

Beer contains female hormones
Last month, Wits University and RAU scientists released the results of a recent analysis that revealed the presence of female hormones in beer.

Men should take a concerned look at their beer consumption. The theory is that beer contains female hormones.

Hops contains phytoestrogens and that by drinking enough beer, men turn into women.

To test the theory, 100 men drank 8 pints of beer each within a 1 hour period.

It was then observed that 100% of the test subjects :

1) Argued over nothing.

2) Refused to apologize when obviously wrong.

3) Gained weight.

4) Talked excessively without making sense.

5) Became overly emotional

6) Couldn't drive.

7) Failed to think rationally

8) Had to sit down while urinating.

No further testing was considered necessary.

~~~~~~~~~~

Upon hearing that her elderly grandfather had just passed away, Katie went straight to her grandparent's house to visit her 95-year-old grandmother and comfort her.

When she asked how her grandfather had died, her grandmother replied, 'He had a heart attack while we were making love on Sunday morning.

' Horrified, Katie told her grandmother that 2 people nearly 100 years old having sex would surely be asking for trouble.'Oh no, my dear,' replied granny.

'Many years ago, realizing our advanced age, we figured out the best time to do it was when the church bells would start to ring. It was just the right rhythm. Nice and slow and even. Nothing too strenuous, simply in on the Ding and out on the Dong.'

She paused to wipe away a tear, and continued, 'He'd still be alive if the ice cream truck hadn't come along.

~~~~~~~~~~

Have you ever wondered what the difference between Grandmothers and Grandfathers is?

Well here it is:

A friend, who worked away from home all week, always made a special effort with his family on the weekends.

Every Sunday morning he would take his 7-year old granddaughter out for a drive in the car for some bonding time – just he and his granddaughter.

One particular Sunday however, he had a bad cold and really didn't feel like being up at all. Luckily, his wife came to the rescue and said that she would take their granddaughter out.

When they returned, the little girl anxiously ran upstairs to see her grandfather.

"Well, did you enjoy your ride with grandma?"

"Oh yes, Papa," the girl replied, "and do you know what?"

"We didn't see a single dumb bastard, dip shit or horse's ass anywhere we went today!'

Brings a tear to your eye doesn't it?

~~~~~~~~~~~~~~~

Last week I checked into my hotel in Atlanta
and was a bit lonely. I thought, I'll call one of
those girls you see advertised in
phone books like escorts and such.

I picked up the phone book and found an ad for
a girl calling herself Erogonique, a lovely girl,
bending over in the photo. She had all the right
curves in all the right places, beautiful long
wavy hair, long graceful legs..... well, you get
the picture! I figured, what the heck, give her a
call.

"Hello," the woman says, God, she sounded
sexy. Afraid I would lose my nerve if I hesitated
I rushed right in. "Hi, I hear you give a great
massage and I'd like you to come to my room
and give me one. No, wait, I should be straight
with you. I'm in town all alone and what I really
want is sex. I want it hard, I want it hot and I
want it now. Bring implements, toys, rubber,
leather, whips, everything you've got in your
bag of tricks. We'll go hot and heavy all night;
tie me up, cover me in chocolate syrup
and whipped cream, anything and everything!
Now, how does that sound?"

"That sounds fantastic," she says,
"but you need to press 9 for an outside line.

I can't stay in that hotel again !!

~~~~~~~~~~

An old Italian Mafia Don is dying and he calls his grandson to his bed!

'Lissin-a me. I wanna for you to taka my chrome plated 38 revolver so you will always remember me.'

'But grandpa, I really don't lika guns. Howzabout you leava me your Rolex watch instead?'

'Shuddup an lissin. Somma day you gonna runna da business. you gonna have a beautifula wife, lotsa money, a biga home and maybe a couple a bambinos' 'Somma day you gonna comma home and maybe find you wife inna bed with another man. Whadda you gonna do then....... **pointa to your watch and say 'Times up'?!!!!!!!!!!!**

~~~~~~~~~~

A crusty old Chief Petty Officer found himself at a gala event hosted by a local socialite. There was no shortage of extremely young ladies in attendance, one of whom approached the Chief for conversation.

'Excuse me , Chief, but you seem to be a very serious man. Is something bothering you?'

'Negative, ma'am. Just serious by nature.'

The young lady looked at his awards and decorations and said, 'It looks like you have seen a lot of action.'

'Yes, ma'am, a lot of action.'

The young lady, tiring of trying to start up a conversation, said, 'You know, you should lighten up a little. Relax and enjoy yourself.'

The Chief Petty Officer just stared at her in his serious manner. Finally the young lady said, 'You know, I hope you don't take this the wrong way, but when is the last time you had sex?'

'1955, ma'am'

'Well, there you are. You really need to chill out and quit taking everything so seriously! I mean, no sex since 1955! That's bloody ridiculous! She took his hand and led him to a private room where she proceeded to 'relax' him several times.

Afterwards, panting for breath, she leaned against his bare chest and said, 'Wow, you sure didn't forget much since 1955.'

The Chief Petty Officer, glancing at his watch, said in his serious voice, 'I hope not; it's only

2130 now.'

(Don't you love military time?)

~~~~~~~~~

Subject: Unfulfilled Fantasy

A 71 year old man goes to his doctor and says.
"Doc, I have a problem. My girlfriend is
sleeping over this Friday, My ex-wife is
sleeping over this Saturday and my wife is
coming home Sunday. I need 3 Viagra pills
to satisfy them all".

The doctor says "You know 3 Viagra pills 3
nights in a row is pretty dangerous for a man of
your age. I will give them to you on the
condition that you return to my office on
Monday so that I can check you out."

The man says "You have a deal, Doc."

Monday morning the man returns with his arm
in a sling. The doctor says "what happened"?
The man answered "nobody showed up!"

~~~~~~~~~~~

A senior citizen goes in for his yearly physical
with his wife tagging Along.

When the doctor enters the examination room
he says, "I will need a urine Sample, a stool
sample, and a sperm sample."

The man, being hard of hearing, turns to his wife and asks, "What did he Say?"

The wife yells back to him,

"GIVE HIM YOUR UNDERPANTS"

~~~~~~~~~~

An old retired sailor puts on his old uniform and heads for the docks once more, for old times sake.

He engages a prostitute and takes her up to a room.

He's soon going at it as well as he can for a guy his age, but needing some reassurance, he asks, 'How am I doing?? '

The prostitute replies, 'Well, old sailor, you're doing about three knots

'Three knots?' he asks. 'What's that supposed to mean??'

She says, 'You're knot hard, you're knot in,

and you're knot getting your money back.

~~~~~~~~~~

Drafting Guys over 60----this is funny & obviously written by a Former Soldier-

New Direction for any war: Send Service Vets over 60!

I am over 60 and the Armed Forces thinks I'm too old to track down terrorists. You can't be older than 42 to join the military. They've got the whole thing ass-backwards. Instead of sending 18-year olds off to fight, they ought to take us old guys. You shouldn't be able to join a military unit until you're at least 35.

For starters: Researchers say 18-year-olds think about sex every 10 seconds. Old guys only think about sex a couple of times a day, leaving us more than 28,000 additional seconds per day to concentrate on the enemy.

Young guys haven't lived long enough to be cranky, and a cranky soldier is a dangerous soldier. 'My back hurts! I can't sleep, I'm tired and hungry' We are impatient and maybe letting us kill some asshole that desperately deserves it will make us feel better and shut us up for a while.

An 18-year-old doesn't even like to get up before 10 a.m. Old guys always get up early to pee so what the hell. Besides, like I said, 'I'm tired and can't sleep and since I'm already up, I may as well be up killing some fanatical SOB....

If captured we couldn't spill the beans because we'd forget where we put them. In fact, name, rank, and serial number would be a real stretch.

Boot camp would be easier for old guys. We're used to getting screamed and yelled at and we're used to soft food. We've also developed an appreciation for guns. We've been using them for years as an excuse to get out of the house, away from the screaming and yelling.

They could lighten up on the obstacle course however. I've been in combat and didn't see a single 20-foot wall with rope hanging over the side, nor did I ever do any pushups after completing basic training.

 Actually, the running part is kind of a waste of energy, too. I've never seen anyone outrun a bullet.

An 18-year-old has the whole world ahead of him.. He's still learning to shave, to start up a conversation with a pretty girl. He still hasn't figured out that a baseball cap has a brim to shade his eyes, not the back of his head.

These are all great reasons to keep our kids at home to learn a little more about life before sending them off into harm's way.

Let us old guys track down those dirty rotten coward terrorists. The last thing an enemy would want to see is a couple of million pissed off old farts with attitudes and automatic weapons who know that their best years are already behind them.

How about recruiting Women over 50 ....with PMS !!! You think Men have attitudes !!! Ohhhhhhhhhhhh my Lord!!! If nothing else, put them on border patrol....we will have it secured the first night!

~~~~~~~~~~~~

An illegal alien in Polk County Florida who got pulled over in a routine traffic stop ended up 'executing' the deputy who stopped him. The deputy was shot eight times, including once behind his right ear at close range. Another deputy was wounded and a police dog killed. A state wide manhunt ensued.

The murderer was found hiding in a wooded area with his gun. After he shot at them, SWAT team officers open fired and hit the guy 68 times.

Now here's the kicker:

Naturally, the liberal media went nuts and asked why they shot the poor undocumented immigrant 68 times.

Sheriff Grady Judd told the Orlando Sentinel:

'Because that's all the ammunition we had.'

Talk about an all-time classic answer.

~~~~~~~~~~~~

A chicken farmer stopped in local bar, sat next to a woman and ordered a glass of champagne.

The woman perked up and said, 'How about that? I just ordered a glass of champagne, too!'

'What a coincidence' the farmer said. 'This is a special day for me ... I am celebrating.'

'This is a special day for me too, I am also celebrating,' said the woman.

'What a coincidence!' said the farmer.

As they clinked glasses he added, 'What are you celebrating?'

'My husband and I have been trying to have a child and today my gynecologist told me that at last I am pregnant!'

'What a coincidence!' said the man, 'I'm a chicken farmer and for years all of my hens were infertile, but today they are all laying fertilized eggs.'

'That's great!' said the woman, 'How did your chickens become fertile?'

'I used a different Cock' he replied,

The woman smiled, clinked his glass and said, 'What a coincidence!'

~~~~~~~~~~

A Bit of History

The US standard railroad gauge (distance
between the rails) is 4 feet, 8.5 inches. That's
an exceedingly odd number.

Why was that gauge used? Because that's the
way they built them in England , and English
expatriates built the US railroads.
Why did the English build them like that?
Because the first rail lines were built by the
same people who built the pre-railroad
tramways, and that's the gauge they used.
Why did 'they' use that gauge then? Because
the people who built the tramways used the
same jigs and tools that they used for building
wagons, which used that wheel spacing.
Why did the wagons have that particular odd
wheel spacing? Well, if they tried to use any
other spacing, the wagon wheels would break
on some of the old, long distance roads
in England , because that's the spacing of the
wheel ruts.

So who built those old rutted roads?
Imperial Rome built the first long distance
roads in Europe (and England) for their
legions. The roads have been used ever since.
And the ruts in the roads? Roman war chariots
formed the initial ruts, which everyone else had
to match for fear of destroying their wagon
wheels. Since the chariots were made
for Imperial Rome, they were all alike in the

matter of wheel spacing. Therefore the United States standard railroad gauge of 4 feet, 8.5 inches is derived from the original specifications for an Imperial Roman war chariot.

Bureaucracies live forever.

So the next time you find a specification/procedure/process and wonder 'What horse's ass came up with it?', you may be exactly right.
Imperial Roman army chariots were made just wide enough to accommodate the rear ends of two war horses. (Two horse's asses.) Now, the twist to the story:

When you see a Space Shuttle sitting on its launch pad, there are two big booster rockets attached to the sides of the main fuel tank. These are solid rocket boosters, or SRB's. The SRB's are made by Thiokol at their factory in Utah . The engineers who designed the SRB's would have preferred to make them a bit fatter, but the SRB's had to be shipped by train from the factory to the launch site. The railroad line from the factory happens to run through a tunnel in the mountains, and the SRB's had to fit through that tunnel. The tunnel is slightly wider than the railroad track, and the railroad track, as you now know, is about as wide as two horses' behinds.

So, a major Space Shuttle design feature of what is arguably the world's most advanced transportation system was determined over two thousand years ago by the width of a horse's ass.

And you thought being a horse's ass wasn't important? Ancient horse's asses control almost everything... and CURRENT Horses Asses are controlling everything else.

~~~~~~~~~~

A blonde was shopping at Target and came across a shiny silver Thermos. She was quite fascinated by it, so she picked it up and took It to the clerk to ask what it was.

The clerk said, 'Why, that's a thermos..... It keeps hot things hot, And cold things cold.'

'Wow, said the blonde, 'that's amazing.....I'm going to buy it!' So she Bought the thermos and took it to work the next day.

Her boss saw it on her desk. 'What's that,' he asked?

'Why, that's a thermos..... It keeps hot things hot and cold things Cold,' she replied..

Her boss inquired, 'What do you have in it?'

The blond replied..... ...'Two popsicles and some coffee.'

~~~~~~~~~~

BEER

What makes white men think they can dance !!

~~~~~~~~~~

Polite Way To Pee...

During one of her daily classes, a teacher trying to teach good manners, asked her students the following question:

'Michael, if you were on a date having dinner with a nice young lady, how would you tell her that you have to go to the bathroom?'

Michael said, 'Just a minute I have to go pee.' The teacher responded by saying, 'That would be rude and impolite.'

'What about you, Sherman, how would you say it?'

Sherman said, 'I am sorry , but I really need to go to the bathroom. I'll be right back..'
'That's better, but it's still not very nice to say the word bathroom at the dinner table.'

'And you, little Johnny, can you use your brain for once and show us your good manners?'

'I would say, 'Darling, may I please be excused for a moment? I have to shake hands with a very dear friend of mine, to whom I hope to introduce you after dinner."

The teacher fainted.

~~~~~~~~~~

T-G-I-F vs. S-H-I-T

A business man got on an elevator.

When he entered, there was a blonde already inside who greeted him with a bright,

"T-G-I-F."

He smiled at her and replied, "S-H-I-T."

She looked puzzled and repeated, "T-G-I-F," more slowly.

He again answered, "S-H-I-T."

The blonde was trying to keep it friendly, so she smiled her biggest smile, and said as sweetly as possibly, "T-G-I-F."

The man smiled back to her and once again, "S-H-I-T."

The exasperated blonde finally decided to explain.

'T-G-I-F' means 'Thank Goodness It's Friday.' Get it, duuhhh?"

The man answered, "'S-H-I-T' means 'Sorry, Honey, It's Thursday -- duuhhh

~~~~~~~~~~

Taliban Mine Sweeping

It was reported today that the Taliban
are using sheep to detect mines.

They send the sheep into a field, and if they're
blown up they have dinner.

If they make it through alive,
they have a date.

Works perfectly....

~~~~~~~~~~

Morris and his wife Esther went to the state fair
every year, And every year Morris would say,

'Esther, I'd like to ride in that helicopter.'
Esther always replied,

'I know Morris, but that helicopter ride is fifty
dollars, And fifty dollars is fifty dollars'

One year Esther and Morris went to the fair,
and Morris said,

'Esther, I'm 85 years old. If I don't ride that
helicopter, I might never get another chance.'

To this, Esther replied, 'Morris that helicopter
ride is fifty dollars, and fifty dollars is fifty
dollars.'

The pilot overheard the couple and said,

'Folks I'll make you a deal. I'll take the both of you for a ride. If you can stay quiet for the entire ride and don't say a word I won't charge you a penny!

But if you say one word it's fifty dollars.'

Morris and Esther agreed and up they went.

The pilot did all kinds of fancy maneuvers, but not a word was heard. He did his daredevil tricks over and over again,

But still not a word.

When they landed, the pilot turned to Morris and said, 'By golly, I did everything I could to get you to yell out, but you didn't.

I'm impressed!'

Morris replied, 'Well, to tell you the truth,

I almost said something when Esther fell out,

But you know, fifty dollars is fifty dollars!'....

~~~~~~~~~~

Women are like phones:

They like to be held, talked to, and touched often.

But push the wrong button and your ass is disconnected.

~~~~~~~~~~

The perfect dentist
A guy and a girl meet at a bar. They get along so well that they decide to go to the girl's place. A few drinks later, the guy takes off his shirt and then washes his hands. He then takes off his trousers and washes his hands again. The girl has been watching him and says,
'You must be a dentist.'
The guy, surprised, says 'Yes....how did you figure that out?'
'Easy,' she replied, 'you keep washing your hands..'

One thing led to another and they make love. After they are done, the girl says, 'You must be a really good dentist.'
The guy, now with a boosted ego says 'Sure, I'm a good dentist, how did you figure that out?'
She replies 'I Didn't Feel a Thing...

~~~~~~~~~~

The sharing of marriage..._

The old man placed an order for one hamburger, French fries and a drink.

He unwrapped the plain hamburger and carefully cut it in half, placing one half in front of his wife.

He then carefully counted out the French fries, dividing them into two piles and neatly placed one pile in front of his wife.

He took a sip of the drink, his wife took a sip and then set the cup down between them . As he began to eat his few bites of hamburger, the people around them were looking over and whispering.

Obviously they were thinking, 'That poor old couple - all they can afford is one meal for the two of them.'

As the man began to eat his fries a young man came to the table and politely offered to buy another meal for the old couple. The old man said, they were just fine - they were used to sharing everything

People closer to the table noticed the little old lady hadn't eaten a bite. She sat there watching her husband eat and occasionally taking turns sipping the drink.

Again, the young man came over and begged them to let him buy another meal for them. This time the old woman said 'No, thank you, we are used to sharing everything.'

Finally, as the old man finished and was wiping his face neatly with the napkin, the young man again came over to the little old lady who had yet to eat a single bite of food and asked 'What is it you are waiting for?'

She answered --

'THE TEETH.'

~~~~~~~~~~

During church service the small children were invited to stand up in front and to say a short prayer to ask for help for something for anyone besides for themselves.

Below is one of those heartfelt sweet prayers:

Dear God:

This year please send clothes for all those poor women in Daddy's computer.

~~~~~~~~~~

Two good ol' boys in a St. Louis trailer park were sitting around talking one afternoon over a cold beer after getting off of work at their local Nissan plant.

After a while the 1st guy says to the 2nd, 'If'n I was to sneak over to your trailer Saturday & make love to your wife while you was off huntin' and she got pregnant and had a baby, would that make us kin?'

The 2nd guy crooked his head sideways for a minute, scratched his head, and squinted his eyes thinking real hard about the question. Finally, he says, 'Well, I don't know about kin, but it would make us even.

~~~~~~~~~~

Jane was sitting in anatomy class on day when her teacher asked her a question. He inquired, "What grows to 10 times its original size when excited?"

Jane blushed and said that she didn't know. Jimmy raised his hand and said, "I know! The pupil of the eye." The teacher replied, "Yes, very good Jimmy."

The teacher turned to Jane and said, "Jane I have three things to say to you: One -- you have a very dirty mind. Two -- you haven't been studying hard enough. And three -- you're going to be very disappointed!"

~~~~~~~~~~

Jacob, age 92, and Rebecca, age 89, living in Florida , are all excited about their decision to get married. They go for a stroll to discuss the wedding, and on the way they pass a drugstore. Jacob suggests they go in.

*Jacob addresses the man behind the counter: "Are you the owner?"

The pharmacist answers, "Yes."
*Jacob: "We're about to get married. Do you sell heart medication?"
Pharmacist: "Of course we do."

*Jacob: "How about medicine for circulation?"
Pharmacist: "All kinds "

*Jacob: "Medicine for rheumatism?"
Pharmacist: "Definitely."

*Jacob: "How about suppositories?"
Pharmacist: "You bet!"

*Jacob: "Medicine for memory problems, arthritis and Alzheimer's?"
Pharmacist: "Yes, a large variety. The works."

*Jacob: "What about vitamins, sleeping pills, Geritol, antidotes for Parkinson's disease?"
Pharmacist: "Absolutely."

*Jacob: "Everything for heartburn and indigestion?"
Pharmacist: "We sure do."

*Jacob: "You sell wheelchairs and walkers and canes?"
Pharmacist: "All speeds and sizes."

*Jacob: "Adult diapers?"
Pharmacist: "Sure."

*Jacob: "We'd like to use this store as our Bridal Registry."

~~~~~~~~~~

Two little kids are in a hospital, lying on stretchers next to each other outside the operating room.
The first kid leans over and asks, "What are you in here for?"

The second kid says, "I'm in here to get my tonsils out and I'm a little nervous."
The first kid says, "You've got nothing to worry about. I had that done when I was four. They put you to sleep, and when you wake up they give you lots of Jello and ice cream. It's a breeze.
"The second kid then asks, "What are you here for?"
The first kid says, "A circumcision."
"Whoa!" the second kid replies. "Good luck buddy. I had that done when I was born. Couldn't walk for a year."

~~~~~~~~~~

Golf Quotes

I was three over. One over a house, one over a patio, and one over a swimming pool.
   ~ George Brett

Actually, the only time I ever took out a one-iron was to kill a tarantula. And I took a 7 to do that..
   ~ Jim Murray

The only sure rule in golf is - he who has the fastest cart never has to play the bad lie.
   ~ Mickey Mantle

Sex and golf are the two things you can enjoy even if you're not good at them.
   ~ Kevin Costner

I don't fear death, but I sure don't like those three-footers for par.
~ Chi Chi Rodriguez

After all these years, it's still embarrassing for me to play on the American golf tour. Like the time I asked my caddie for a sand wedge and he came back ten minutes later with a ham on rye..
~ Chi Chi Rodriguez

The ball retriever is not long enough to get my putter out of the tree.
~ Brian Weis

Swing hard in case you hit it.
~ Dan Marino

My favorite shots are the practice swing and the conceded putt. The rest can never be mastered.
~ Lord Robertson

Give me golf clubs, fresh air and a beautiful partner, and you can keep the clubs and the fresh air.
~ Jack Benny

There is no similarity between golf and putting; they are two different games, one played in the air, and the other on the ground.
~ Ben Hogan

Professional golf is the only sport where, if you win 20% of the time, you're the best.
~ Jack Nicklaus

If you watch a game, it's fun. If you play at it, it's recreation. If you work at it, it's golf.
~ Bob Hope

While playing golf today I hit two good balls. I stepped on a rake.
~ Henry Youngman

If you think it's hard to meet new people, try picking up the wrong golf ball.
~ Jack Lemmon

You can make a lot of money in this game. Just ask my ex-wives. Both of them are so rich that neither of their husbands work.
~ Lee Trevino

I'm not saying my golf game went bad, but if I grew tomatoes, they'd come up sliced.
~ Lee Trevino

~~~~~~~~~~

POST COMPETITION ASKING FOR A TWO-LINE RHYME WITH THE MOST ROMANTIC FIRST LINE, AND THE LEAST ROMANTIC SECOND LINE:

1. My darling, my lover, my beautiful wife:
Marrying you has screwed up my life.

2. My love, you take my breath away.
What have you stepped in to smell this way?

3. Kind, intelligent, loving and hot;

81

This describes everything you are not.

4. Love may be beautiful, love may be bliss,
But I only slept with you 'cause I was pissed.

5. I thought that I could love no other
-- that is until I met your brother.

6. Roses are red, violets are blue, sugar is
sweet, and so are you.
But the roses are wilting, the violets are dead,
the sugar bowl's Empty and so is your head.

7. I want to feel your sweet embrace;
But don't take that paper bag off your face.

8. I love your smile, your face, and your eyes
Damn, I'm good at telling lies!

9. I see your face when I am dreaming.
That's why I always wake up screaming.

10. My feelings for you no words can tell,
Except for maybe 'Go to hell.'

11. What inspired this amorous rhyme?
Two parts vodka, one part lime.

~~~~~~~~~~

Manure: In the 16th and 17th centuries,
everything had to be transported by ship, and it
was also before commercial fertilizer's
invention, so large shipments of manure

were common. It was shipped dry, because in dry form it weighed a lot less than when wet, but once water (at sea) hit it, it not only became heavier, but the process of fermentation began again, of which a byproduct is methane gas.   As the stuff was stored below decks in bundles, you can see what could (and did) happen.

Methane began to build up below decks, and the first time someone came below at night with a lantern, BOOOOM! Several ships were destroyed in this manner before it was determined just what was happening.

After that, the bundles of manure were always stamped with the term 'Ship High In Transit' on them, which meant for the sailors to stow it high enough off of the lower decks so that any water that came into the hold would not touch this volatile cargo and start the production of methane.
Thus evolved the term 'S.H.I.T.' , (Ship High In Transport) which has come down through the centuries and is in use to this very
Day.   You probably did not know the true history of this word.   Neither did I.

I had always thought it was a golfing term.

~~~~~~~~~~

Men are like fine wine. They all start out like grapes, and it is our job to stomp on them and keep them in the dark until they mature into something you'd like to have dinner with.

~~~~~~~~~~

I was lonely and decided life would be more fun if I had a pet. So I went to the pet store and told the owner that I wanted to buy an unusual Pet.

After some discussion, I finally decided to buy a centipede.

The little 100 legged bug came with a little white box to use for his house. So cute!

I took the box home, found a good location for the box, and decided I would start off by taking my new Pet to the bar for a drink. So I asked the centipede in the box, "Would you like to go to Frank's place with me and have a beer?" Silence; there was no answer. This bothered him a bit, so I waited a few minutes, and then asked him again, "How about going to the bar and having a beer with me?" Again, there was no answer, nothing but silence.. So, I waited a few minutes more, thinking about the situation. I decided to ask him one more time. This time, putting my face up against the centipede's house and shouting, "Hey, in there! Would you like to go to Frank's place and have a beer with me?"

A little voice came out of the box: "I heard you the first time! I'm putting my shoes on!

~~~~~~~~~~

Two medical students were walking along the street when they saw an old man walking with his legs apart. He was stiff legged and walking slowly.

One of the students said to his friend, 'I'm sure the poor old man has Petry Syndrome. Those people walk just like that.'

The other student said, 'No, I don't think so. The old man surely has Zovitzki Syndrome. He walks slowly and his legs are apart just as we learned in class.'

Since they couldn't agree they decided to ask the old man. They approached him and one of the students said to him, 'We're medical students and couldn't help but notice the way you walk, but we couldn't agree on the syndrome you might have. Could you tell us what it is?'

The old man said, 'I'll tell you, but first you must tell me what you two fine medical students think.' One of the students said, 'I think it's Petry Syndrome.' The old man said, 'You thought... but you are wrong.'
Then the other student said, 'I think you have Zovitzki Syndrome.'

The old man said, 'You thought...... but you are also wrong.'

So they asked him, 'Well, old timer, what do you have?' The old man said, 'I thought it was GAS... but I was wrong too.'

~~~~~~~~~~~

An old Ukrainian about 80 years old lived alone in Edmonton. He wanted to plant his annual tomato garden, but it was very difficult work, as the ground was very hard to turn over for an 80 year old. His only son, Walter, who used to help him, was in prison in Prince Albert, Saskatchewan penitentiary for an extended sentence.
The old man wrote a letter to his son and described his predicament:

Dear Walter,
I am feeling pretty sad, because it looks like I won't be able to plant my tomato garden this year. I'm just getting too old to be digging up a garden plot. I know if you were here, my troubles would be over. I know you would be happy to dig the plot for me, like in the old days.   Love Tato .

A few days later he received a letter from his son.
Dear Tato,
Don't dig up that garden. That's where the

bodies are buried. Love Walter.

At 4 a.m. the next morning, RCMP and local Edmonton police arrived and dug up the entire backyard area without finding any bodies. They finally apologized to the old man and left. That same day the old man received another letter from his son.

Dear Tato,
Go ahead and plant the tomatoes now. That's the best I could do under the circumstances. Love you Walter.

~~~~~~~~~~~~~~

In a recent survey carried out for a leading toiletries firm 'Brut', people from Detroit have proved to be the most likely to have had sex in the shower.

In the survey, 86% of Detroit's inner city residents said that they have enjoyed sex in the shower.

The other 14% said they hadn't been to prison yet.

~~~~~~~~~~~~~~

13 Things PMS Stands For:

1. Pass My Shotgun

2. Psychotic Mood Shift

3. Perpetual Munching Spree

4. Puffy Mid-Section

5. People Make me Sick

6. Provide Me with Sweets

7 Pardon My Sobbing

8. Pimples May Surface

9. Pass My Sweat pants

10. Pissy Mood Syndrome

11. Plainly; Men Suck

12. Pack My Stuff

and my favoriteone :

13. Potential Murder Suspect

~~~~~~~~~~

Towards the end of the golf course, Dave hit his ball into the woods and found it in a patch of pretty yellow buttercups. Trying to get his ball back in play, he ended up trashing just about every buttercup in the patch.

All of a sudden.....POOF!! In a flash and puff of smoke, a little old woman appeared.

She said, "I'm Mother Nature! Do you know how long it took me to make those buttercups? Just for doing what you have done, you won't have any butter for your popcorn for the rest of your life: better still, you won't have any butter for your toast for the rest of your life...... As a matter of fact, you'll never have any butter for anything the rest of your life!!!!!

Then POOF!......she was gone!

After Dave recovered from the shock, he hollered for his friend, "Fred, where are you?"

Fred yells back "I'm over here in the pussy willows."

Dave shouts back, "DON'T SWING, Fred; FOR THE LOVE OF GOD, DON'T SWING!"

~~~~~~~~~~

A man was driving when a traffic camera flashed. He thought his picture was taken for exceeding the speed limit, even though he knew he was not speeding. Just to be sure, he went around the block and passed the same spot, driving even more slowly, but again the camera flashed. He thought this was quite funny, so he slowed down even further as he drove past the area, but the traffic camera flashed yet again. He tried a fourth time with the same result. The fifth time he was laughing when the camera flashed as he rolled past at a snail's pace.

Two weeks later, he got five traffic fine letters in the mail for driving without a seat belt.

And we think Blonde girls are dumb.

~~~~~~~~~~

A blonde goes into work one morning crying her eyes out.

Her boss asked sympathetically, 'What's the matter?'

The blonde replies, 'Early this morning I got a phone call saying that My mother had passed away.'

The boss, feeling sorry for her, says, 'Why don't you go home for the Day? Take the day off to relax and rest.'

'Thanks, but I'd be better off here. I need to keep my mind off it and I have the best chance of doing that here.'

The boss agrees and allows the blonde to work

as usual. A couple of hours pass and the boss decides to check on the blonde. He looks out from his office and sees the blonde crying hysterically.

'What's so bad now? Are you gonna be okay?' he asks.

'No!' exclaims the blonde. 'I just received a horrible call from my sister. Her mother died, too!'

~~~~~~~~~~

Walking into the bar, Mike said to Charlie the bartender, "Pour me a stiff one - just had another fight with the little woman."

"Oh yeah?" said Charlie. "And how did this one end?"

"When it was over," Mike replied, "she came to me on her hands and knees."

"Really? Now that's a switch! What did she say?"

She said, "Come out from under the bed, you little chicken-shit."

~~~~~~~~~~

"Life should NOT be a journey to the grave with the intention of arriving safely in an attractive and well preserved body, but rather to skid in sideways, chocolate in one hand,

martini in the other with your body thoroughly
used up, totally worn out and screaming
"WOO HOO what a ride!"

~~~~~~~~~~~

RETIREMENT BONUS

If this doesn't make you laugh, you are truly
humor impaired!

The Navy found they had too many officers
and decided to offer an early retirement
bonus...

They promised any officer who volunteered for
Retirement a bonus of $1,000 for every inch
measured in a straight line between any
Two points in his body.

The officer got to choose what those two points
would be.

The first officer who accepted asked that he be
measured from the top of His head to the tip of
his toes.

He was measured at six feet and walked out
with a bonus of $72,000.

The second officer who accepted was a little
smarter and asked to be measured from the tip
of his outstretched hands to his toes.

He walked Out with $96,000.

The third one was a noncommissioned officer, a grizzly old Chief who, when asked where he would like to be measured replied,
'From the tip of my weenie to my testicles.'

It was suggested by the pension man that he might want to reconsider, explaining about the nice big checks the previous two Officers had received.

But the old Chief insisted and they decided to go along with him providing the measurement was taken by a Medical Officer.

The Medical Officer arrived and instructed the Chief to 'drop 'em,' which He did. The medical officer placed the tape measure on the tip of the Chief's weenie and began to work back. Dear Lord!' he suddenly exclaimed, 'Where Are your testicles?'

The old Chief calmly replied, ' Vietnam

~~~~~~~~~~

If you've ever worked for a boss that reacts before getting the facts and thinking things through, you will love this!

Arcelor-Mittal Steel, feeling it was time for a shakeup, hired a new CEO.

The new boss was determined to rid the company of all slackers.

On a tour of the facilities, the CEO noticed a guy leaning against the wall with his hands in his pockets.

The room was full of workers and he wanted to let them know that he meant business.

He walked up to the guy leaning against the wall and asked, 'How much money do you make a week?'

A little surprised, the young man looked at him and replied, 'I make $400 a week. Why?'

The CEO then handed the guy $1,600 in cash and screamed, 'Here's four weeks' pay, now GET OUT And don't come back.'

Feeling pretty good about himself, the CEO looked around the room and asked, 'Does anyone want to tell me what that goof-ball did here? '

From across the room came a voice, 'He's the pizza delivery guy from Domino's.

~~~~~~~~~~

The trouble with some women is that they get all excited about nothing and then they marry him.

~~~~~~~~~~

My neighbor found out her dog could hardly hear so she took it to her veterinarian. He found that the problem was hair in its ears, so he cleaned both ears and the dog could hear fine.

The vet then proceeded to tell her that if she wanted to keep this from recurring she should go to the store and get some "Nair" hair remover and rub it in the dog's ears once a month.

The lady goes to the drug store to get some "Nair" hair remover.

At the register the druggist tells her, "If you're going to use this under your arms, don't use deodorant for a few days."

She replies: "I'm not using it under my arms.."

The druggist responds: "If you're using it on your legs, don't shave for a couple of days."

She says: "I'm not using it on my legs either; if you must know, I'm using it on my schnauzer."

The druggist replies: "Then stay off your bicycle for a week."

~~~~~~~~~~~

Bubbles and Barbie, two blonde sisters
had promised their Uncle,   who had been a
seafaring gentleman all his life, to bury him at
sea   when he died. Of course, in due time, he
did pass away and the two blondes kept their
promise.

They set off from Clearwater Beach with their
uncle all stitched up in a burial bag and loaded
him onto their rowboat.

 After a while Bubbles says, 'Do you think we're
out far enough, Barbie?'

 Barbie slipped over the side and finding the
water only knee deep said, 'Nope, not yet
Bubbles.'

 So they row a little farther.... Again Bubbles
ask Barbie, 'Do you think we're out far enough
now?'

Once again Barbie slips over the side and
almost immediately says, 'No, this will never
do. The water is only up to my chest.'

So on they row and row and row, and finally
Barbie slips over the side and disappears.
Quite a bit of time goes by and poor Bubbles is
really getting worried when suddenly
Barbie breaks the surface, gasping for breath
she says, 'OK, it's finally deep enough. Hand
 me the shovel.'

~~~~~~~~~~

There were three blonde pregnant women sitting together. The first woman said, "I'm going to have a boy."
"How did you know that?" the other two women asked her.
"Because I was on top," she replied.
The second pregnant woman said, "I'm going to have a girl."
"How did you know that?" asked the other two women.
"Because I was on the bottom."
Then the third pregnant woman started to cry. What's wrong?" the two other women asked her.
"She replied, "I'm going to have a puppy!"

~~~~~~~~~~

Patients needing blood transfusions may benefit from receiving **chicken blood** rather than human blood. It tends to make the men more cocky and the women lay better.!!!!!!
Just thought you'd like to know.

~~~~~~~~~

Polish Sausage

Everyone is in a hurry to scream 'racism' these days!

'In what aisle could I find the Polish sausage?' The clerk looks at him and says, 'Are you Polish?'

The guy (clearly offended) says, 'Well, yes I am. But let me ask you something.

If I had asked for Italian sausage, would you ask me if I was Italian?

Or if I had asked for German Bratwurst, would you ask me if I was German?

Or if I asked for a kosher hot dog, would you ask me if I was Jewish?

Or if I had asked for a taco, would you ask if I was Mexican?'

'If I asked for some Irish whiskey, would you ask if I was Irish?'

The clerk says, 'Well, no, I probably wouldn't!'

With deep self-righteous indignation, the guy says, 'Well then, why did you ask me if I'm Polish because I asked for Polish sausage?'

The clerk replied, 'Because you're in Home Depot'

~~~~~~~~~~

Seamus and Murphy fancied a pint or two but didn't have a lot of money between them, they could only raise the staggering sum of one Euro.

Murphy said 'Hang on, I have an idea.'

He went next door to the butcher's shop and came out with one large sausage.

Shamus said 'Are you crazy? Now we don't have any money at all!'

Murphy replied, 'Don't worry - just follow me .'

He went into the pub where he immediately ordered two pints of Guinness and two glasses of Jamieson Whisky.

Seamus said 'Now you've lost it. Do you know how much trouble we will be in? We haven't got any money!!'

Murphy replied, with a smile. 'Don't worry, I have a plan , Cheers! '

They downed their Drinks. Murphy said, 'OK, I'll stick the sausage through my zipper and you go on your knees and put it in your mouth.'

The barman noticed them, went berserk, and threw them out.

They continued this, pub after pub, getting more and more drunk, all for free.

At the tenth pub Seamus said 'Murphy - I don't think I can do any more of this. I'm drunk and me knees are killing me !'

Murphy said, 'How do you think I feel? I can't

even remember which pub I lost the sausage in.'

~~~~~~~~~~

Three cowboys were seated around the campfire out on the lonesome prairie. They were the strongest of the strong and the bravest of the brave and they wanted to prove it to each other.

Tom, the hand from Idaho, said, 'I must be the strongest, meanest, toughest cowboy there is. Why, just the other day, a bull got loose in the corral. It had gored six men before I wrestled it to the ground by the horns with my bare hands and castrated that sucker with my teeth.'

Bern from Wyoming, couldn't stand to be bested, 'That's nothing. I was walking down the trail yesterday and a seven-foot diamondback rattler slid out from under a rock and made a move for me. I grabbed that bastard with my bare hands, bit off its head, and sucked the poison down in one gulp. I didn't even get a belly ache.'

Bob, the cowboy from Texas, remained silent but slowly stirred the campfire coals with his pecker.

~~~~~~~~~~

This morning as I was buttoning my shirt, a

button fell off. After that, I picked up my briefcase, and the handle fell off.

Then I went to open the door, and the doorknob fell off. I went to get into my car, and the door handle came off in my hand.

Now I'm terrified, I have to go pee.....!

~~~~~~~~~~

One day a father on his way home from work suddenly remembers that it's his daughter's birthday.

He pulls over to a Toy Shop and asks the salesperson, 'How much for one of those Barbie's in the display window?'

The salesperson answers, 'Which one do you mean, Sir?

"We have: Work Out Barbie , Shopping Barbie , Beach Barbie, Disco Barbie , Ballerina Barbie, Astronaut Barbie, Skater Barbie all priced at $19.95, and Divorced Barbie for $265.95'.

The amazed father asks: 'It 's what?! Why is the Divorced Barbie $265.95 and the others only $19.95?'

The annoyed salesperson rolls her eyes, sighs, and answers:
'Sir..., Divorced Barbie comes with: Ken's Car, Ken's House, Ken's Boat, Ken's Furniture,

Ken's Computer, one of Ken's Friends,
and a key chain made with Ken's balls.

~~~~~~~~~~

The doctor, after an examination, sighed and
said, 'I've got some bad news. You have
cancer, and you'd best put your affairs in
order.'

The woman was shocked, but managed to
compose herself and walk into the waiting
room where her daughter had been waiting.

'Well, daughter, we women celebrate when
things are good, and we celebrate when things
don't go so well. In this case, things aren't
well. I have cancer. So, let's head to the club
and have a martini.'

After 3 or 4 martinis, the two were feeling a
little less somber. There were some laughs and
more martinis. They were eventually
approached by some of the woman's old
friends, who were curious as to what the two
were celebrating.

The woman told her friends they were drinking
to her impending end, 'I've been diagnosed
with AIDS.'

The friend s were aghast, gave the woman
their condolences and beat a hasty retreat.

After the friends left, the woman's daughter

leaned over and whispered, 'Momma, I thought you said you were dying of cancer, and you just told your friends you were dying of AIDS! Why did you do that??'

'Because I don't want any of those bitches sleeping with your father after I'm gone.'

And THAT, my friends, is what is called, 'Putting Your Affairs In Order.'

~~~~~~~~~~

It has been determined, the most used sexual position for married couples is a doggie position.

The husband sits up and begs.
The wife rolls over and plays dead...

~~~~~~~~~~

Two women friends had gone for a girl's night out. Both were very faithful and loving wives, however they had gotten over-enthusiastic on the Bacardi Breezers.

Incredibly drunk and walking home they needed to pee, so they stopped in the cemetery.

One of them had nothing to wipe with so she thought she would take off her panties and use them.

Her friend however was wearing a rather expensive pair of panties and did not want to ruin them.

She was lucky enough to squat down next to a grave that had a wreath with a ribbon on it, so she proceeded to wipe with that.

After the girls did their business they proceeded to go home.

The next day one of the women's husband was concerned that his normally sweet and innocent wife was still in bed hung over, so he phoned the other husband and said:
'These girl nights out have got to stop! I'm starting to suspect the worst. .. my wife came home with no panties!!'

'That's nothing' said the other husband,
'Mine came back with a card stuck to her butt that said.....
" From all of us at the Fire Station. "We'll never forget you.

~~~~~~~~~~

The Dentist pulls out a freezing needle to give the man a shot.
'No way! No needles! I hate needles,' the patient said.
The Dentist starts to hook up the laughing gas and the man objects.
'I can't do the gas thing. The thought of having

the gas mask on is suffocating me!'
The Dentist then asks the patient if he has any objection to taking a pill.
'No objection,' the patient says. 'I'm fine with pills.'
The Dentist then returns and says, 'Here's a Viagra tablet.'
The patient says, 'Wow! I didn't know Viagra worked as a painkiller!!!'
'It doesn't,' said the Dentist, 'but it will give you something to hold onto when I pull your tooth.'

~~~~~~~~~~~

Two Irishmen were sitting in a pub having beer and watching the brothel across the street. They saw a Baptist minister walk into the brothel, and one of them said, "Aye, 'tis a shame to see a man of the cloth goin' bad."

Then they saw a Rabbi enter the brothel, and the other Irishman said, "Aye, 'tis a shame to see that the Jews are falling' victim to temptation."

Then they saw a Catholic priest enter the brothel, and one of the Irishmen said, "What a terrible pity, one of the girls must be quite ill."

~~~~~~~~~~~

An Irishman arrived at J.FK Airport and wandered around the terminal with tears streaming down his cheeks.

An airline employee asked him if he was
already homesick.
"No,"replied the Irishman.
"I've lost all me luggage!"
"How'd that happen?"
"The cork fell out!"said the Irishman.

~~~~~~~~~~

McQuillan walked into a bar and ordered
martini after martini, each time removing the
olives and placing them in a jar.

When the jar was filled with olives and all the
drinks consumed, the Irishman started to
leave.
"S'cuse me",said a customer, who was puzzled
over what McQuillan had done,
"what was that all about?"�

"Nothin', said the Irishman,
"me wife just sent me out for a jar of olives!"

~~~~~~~~~~

A Blonde goes over to her friend's house
wearing a T.G.I.F.Tee-shirt.

'Why are you wearing a Thank God It's Friday
tee-shirt on Monday?'

'Oh crap!' the blonde says. 'I didn't realize it
was a religious T-shirt.

I thought it meant Tits Go In Front.'

~~~~~~~~~~

A little 4 year old boy was running through the house when all of a sudden he stopped and said "Oppps"..

He turned around with a big sheepish grin on his face and said "Grammy, I just burped from my bottom.

~~~~~~~~~~

A crusty old biker, on a summer ride in the country, walks into a tavern and sees a sign hanging over the bar, which reads:

CHEESEBURGER: $1.50
CHICKEN SANDWICH: $2.50
HAND JOB: $500.00

Checking his wallet for the necessary payment, he walks up to the bar and beckons to the exceptionally attractive female bartender serving drinks to a meager looking group of farmers.

'Yes,' she inquires with a knowing smile, 'can I help you?'

'I was wondering,' whispers the old biker, 'are you the young lady who gives the hand-jobs?

'Yes, she smiles and purrs, I sure am.
The old biker replies, 'Well wash your hands. I
want a cheeseburger.'

~~~~~~~~~~

The Seven Dwarfs go to the Vatican, and
because they are the Seven Dwarfs, they are
immediately ushered in to see the
Pope. Grumpy leads the pack.

Grumpy, my son, says the Pope, 'What can I
do for you?'

Grumpy asks, 'Excuse me your Excellency, but
are there any dwarf nuns in Rome?'

The Pope wrinkles his brow at the odd
question, thinks for a moment and answers,
'No, Grumpy, there are no dwarf nuns in
Rome'. In the background, a few of the dwarfs
start giggling. Grumpy turns around and glares,
silencing them.

Grumpy turns back, 'Your Worship, are there
any dwarf nuns in all of Europe?'

The Pope, puzzled now, again thinks for a
moment and then answers, 'No, Grumpy, there
are no dwarf nuns in Europe'.

This time, all of the other dwarfs burst into
laughter. Once again, Grumpy turns around

and silences them with an angry glare.

Grumpy turns back and says, 'Mr. Pope! Are there ANY dwarf nuns anywhere in the world?'

The Pope, really confused by the questions says, 'No, my son, there are no dwarf nuns anywhere in the world.'

The 6 other dwarfs collapse into a heap, rolling and laughing, pounding the floor, tears rolling down their cheeks, as they begin chanting......

Grumpy screwed a penguin!
Grumpy screwed a penguin!

~~~~~~~~~~

Your birth certificate is an apology letter from the condom factory.

A wife is a sex object. Every time you ask for sex, she objects.

Impotence: Nature's way of saying 'No hard feelings...'

There are only two four letter words that are offensive to men - 'don't' and 'stop', unless they are used together.

Panties: Not the best thing on earth, but next to the best thing on earth.

There are three stages of sex in a man's life: Tri Weekly, Try Weekly, and Try Weakly.

Virginity can be cured.

Virginity is not dignity, its lack of opportunity.

Having sex is like playing bridge. If you don't have a good partner, you'd better have a good hand.

I tried phone sex once, but the holes in the dialer were too small.

Marriage is the only war where you get to sleep with the enemy.

What's an Australian kiss?
The same thing as a French kiss, only down under.

A couple just married were happy with the whole thing. He was happy with the Hole and she was happy with the Thing......

What are the three biggest tragedies in a mans life?
Life sucks, job sucks, and the wife doesn't.

Why do men find it difficult to make eye contact?
Breasts don't have eyes.

Despite the old saying, 'Don't take your

troubles to bed', many men still sleep with their wives!!

~~~~~~~~~~

A week after their marriage, the backwoods newlyweds, Ed and Arlene, paid a visit to their doctor.

"You ain't gonna believe this, Doc," said the husband. "My thingy's turnin' blue."

"That's pretty unusual," said the doctor. "Let me examine you."

The doctor takes a look. Sure enough, the redneck's "thingy" really was blue.

The doctor turns to the wife, "Are you using the diaphragm that I prescribed for you?"

"Yep, shore am," she replied brightly.

"And what kind of jelly are you using with it?"

"Grape," she said.

Some Words Of Wisdom From The Author

Some Days you are the pigeon

And other days you are the statue

~~~~~~~~~~~

Let your smile change the world

Don't let the world change your smile

~~~~~~~~~~~

Thank you for reading our joke book.
Please look at our other joke books and feel
free to buy one.

ABOUT THE AUTHOR

Carey has been up and down "The Yellow Brick Road" so many times; he likens his life to a road map.

He has enjoyed every minute of the trip and wouldn't trade his experiences for anything.

Accomplishments

34 copyrights and 4 patent applications
Golfer for 76 years
Practicing tax accountant for 60 years
Bowling Professional for 30 years
Professional football handicapper, 28 years
Nevada Real Estate Broker 10 years
Owned and operated 27 businesses
~

Carey is one of the largest joke book authors on the internet
~

Favorite Saying
If you keep on doing
What you have been doing,
You will keep on getting,
What you have been getting.
(Author Unknown)
~

Author's Favorite Thought
"Change is Inevitable"
~

Dedication
This book is dedicated to his two lovely daughters and their mother who have shared many of the trips along the way.

OTHER BOOKS BY THE AUTHOR

Non Fiction Books
By Carey Erichson

Bowling Ages 7 to 70
Business is a Bitch
The Little Fish That Could
Fairy Tales From the I.R.S.
The Book Of Golf Tips
The Golf Shot Maker
The Rise & Fall of American Family Values
Remarry or Cohabitate

Joke Books By
Carey Erichson

Risque' Jokes Unlimited
I Laughed So Hard I Peed My Panties
Oppppsss I Peed My Panties Again
Jokes Grandma Shouldn't Hear
Grandpa's Naughty Joke Book
Mommy's Dirty Little Secrets
Grandma's Naughty Joke Book
Daddy's Dirty Little Joke Book
The Day My Private Part Died
Where Did My Virginity Go
Where Did My Willie Go
Naughty Jokes For Grown Ups
Risque' Coffee Clatch Jokes
Risque' Adult Joke Book

Let's Offend Everybody
Nice and Naughty Jokes
This Jokes On Me
These Jokes Are Great
What is A Selfie
Our 20th Joke Book
Man Rules vs Woman Rules

www.http://kartines. com

Please visit our company website. We sell the following items and services.

Golf Products
Bowling Products
Joke Books
Children Books
Golf Books
NFL Football Picks
NFL Football Stats
Disabled Walker Products
Income Tax Products

Or call us at:

209-295-7789

Made in the USA
Monee, IL
27 November 2023

47537604R00066